D1139333

 ISLINGTON

Please return this item on or before the last date sta~
be liable to overdue charges. To renew an item call t~
access the online catalogue at www.islington.gov.uk/libraries. You will need
your library membership number and PIN number.

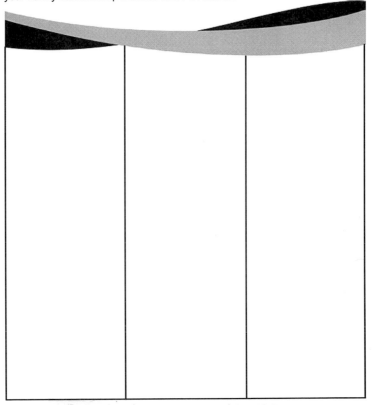

Islington Libraries

020 7527 6900   www.islington.gov.uk/libraries

TEACHER
CREATURES

Franklin Watts
First published in Great Britain in 2018 by The Watts Publishing Group

Text copyright © Tony Lee 2018
Illustration copyright © Marc Ellerby 2018

Illustrator: Marc Ellerby
Design Manager: Peter Scoulding
Cover Designer: Cathryn Gilbert
Production Manager: Robert Dale
Series Consultant: Paul Register
Executive Editor: Adrian Cole

HB ISBN 978 1 4451 5717 7
PB ISBN 978 1 4451 5718 4
Library ebook ISBN 978 1 4451 5719 1

Printed in China

MIX
Paper from
responsible sources
FSC
www.fsc.org
FSC® C104740

Franklin Watts
An imprint of
Hachette Children's Group
Part of The Watts Publishing Group
Carmelite House
50 Victoria Embankment
London EC4Y 0DZ

An Hachette UK Company
www.hachette.co.uk

www.franklinwatts.co.uk

TEACHER
CREATURES

TONY LEE AND MARC ELLERBY

EDGE
FRANKLIN WATTS

LONDON·SYDNEY

SHERIDAN ACADEMY – WEST LONDON

FIRST DAY AT THE **NEW** SCHOOL, NASIR – YOU READY FOR THIS?

NOT REALLY, ASIF – BUT MUM WILL **KILL US IF WE GO BACK!**

WHY ARE THERE NO **STUDENTS** HERE?

I DUNNO – I MEAN, THE LESSONS START IN --

WE USED THE **WRONG TIMETABLE!**

WE'RE LATE!

GREAT START TO DAY ONE!

THE SCHOOL OFFICE.

SHERIDAN ACADEMY

EXCUSE ME - IS THE HEADTEACHER HERE?

WE NEED TO SPEAK TO HER.

IT'S ABOUT TONIGHT'S MEETING.

I DO HOPE THAT YOUR PARENTS ARE COMING.

IT WOULD BE **TERRIBLE** FOR YOU IF THEY CAN'T COME.

BUT IT'S OUR FIRST DAY. WE WEREN'T TOLD.

WE'LL NEED TO CALL THEM.

THEN I SUGGEST YOU DO THAT.

THERE WILL BE **NO** EXCEPTIONS TONIGHT.

← THE HEADTEACHER

≠GULP≠

THE STAFFROOM.

STAFF ONLY

KNOCK! KNOCK!

HELLO? ANYONE HERE?

ARGH!

JUST SOME COATS. SORRY.

CLATTER!

CAN YOU HEAR THAT? THERE'S TALKING IN THE NEXT ROOM.

WE SHOULDN'T BE HERE. STAFFROOMS ARE SACRED TEACHER GROUND. NO STUDENTS WELCOME!

WE SHOULD HAVE EVERY PARENT OF EVERY STUDENT THERE TONIGHT!

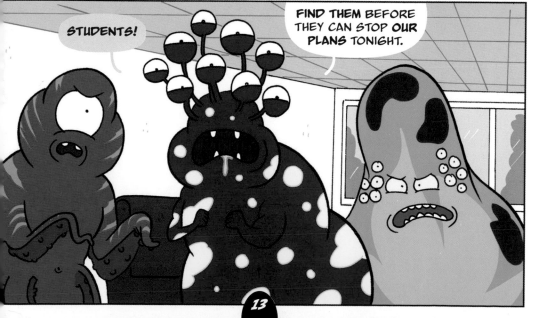

THEY WERE TALKING ABOUT **TONIGHT.** SOMETHING ABOUT THE PARENTS?

IT'S WHY THEY'RE MAKING SURE **EVERY PARENT** TURNS UP TONIGHT.

THEY'RE GOING TO TAKE OVER ALL OF THEIR BODIES! IT'S AN INVASION!

THE ONLY HOPE WE HAVE IS **THIS.**

WHAT IS IT?

I SAW ONE OF THE 'TEACHERS' MIXING SOME **LIQUIDS** IN THE CHEMISTRY LAB.

WHEN SHE SPILLED THE MIXTURE IT TOUCHED HER --

AND SHE **EXPLODED.** POP!

ONCE I WORK OUT HOW TO **COPY** IT - WE CAN STOP THEM ALL!

IN THE CHEMISTRY LAB.

QUICK, BEFORE SOMEONE COMES!

I THINK I'VE GOT IT!

HOW WILL WE KNOW IF IT **WORKS**?

WE WON'T.

GREAT. SO WHAT'S NEXT?

WHAT'S NEXT IS **YOU** ALL SPEND SOME TIME WITH THE HEADTEACHER --

-- AND YOU CAN TELL HER WHY YOU'RE SNEAKING AROUND THE LAB.

SPLAT!

WE'RE UNDER ATTACK! LEAVE THE SKIN SUIT!

THANK YOU --

COULDN'T LET THEM TURN YOU INTO A **HUMAN ONESIE,** COULD WE?

WAIT - YOU'RE EVIL VIKKI, THE BULLY --

IS THAT WHAT PEOPLE CALL ME? WELL, I'M **TRYING** TO MANAGE MY ANGER.

NOW I'M **TRYING TO SAVE WORLD.**

THE **EFFECTS** WERE IMPRESSIVE.

I PREFERRED THE **MUSICAL NUMBER** THE TEACHERS DID LAST YEAR.

LATER.

WE FOUND SOME **STUDENT SUITS** IN THE BASEMENT.

LOOKS LIKE WE **STOPPED** ANOTHER PART OF THEIR PLAN.

HI THERE.

THANKS FOR BELIEVING I COULD DO THAT. NOT MANY PEOPLE BELIEVE IN ME.

MAYBE IF YOU DIDN'T FIRE **MEATBALLS** AT THEIR HEADS?

YEAH, I'LL REMEMBER THAT.

YOU WERE VERY **BRAVE**, NASIR.

IF YOU EVER WANT TO **GRAB A MILKSHAKE** --

OH! UM... SURE!

NASIR! YOU'RE **BLUSHING!**